"*Into The Forest* is a charming way to spark important discussions with children about anxiety and an engaging way to share creative, nature-focused strategies to support wellbeing."

— **Marina Lewis-King**, *Programme Manager, A New Direction (award-winning not-for-profit organisation generating opportunities for children and young people to develop their creativity)*

"*Into The Forest* is a precious story, therapeutic gold, as it weaves in the means of becoming more fully embodied through instinctual and sensory connection. The illustrations are fabulous, as we witness the transformation of the forest through the main character."

— **Molly Wolfe**, *Art Psychotherapist, Sandplay Specialist*

"Learning to be calm and 'in the moment' when experiencing difficult feelings such as loneliness, sadness, worry or fear is a really important core life skill that helps us cope with everyday ups and downs as well as with more stressful situations. This set of three therapeutic fairy stories cleverly explains how we can learn to do this through connecting with nature. A truly wonderful set of resources – of value to us all and in particular to those with emotional or mental health difficulties."

— **Sarah Temple**, *GP and author, www.allemotionsareok.co.uk*

T0056265

Into The Forest

This beautifully illustrated and sensitive fairy tale has been created for children experiencing feelings of anxiety. With engaging and gentle illustrations to help prompt conversation, it tells the story of a boy who is taught by an animal-guide how to live in the present rather than fear the future. This book is also available to buy as part of the *Therapeutic Fairy Tales, Volume 2* set, which includes *The Waves* and *The Sky Fox*.

Therapeutic Fairy Tales Volume 1 (2021) and *Volume 2* are both a series of short, modern tales dedicated to exploring challenging feelings and life situations that might be faced by young children. Each fairy tale is designed to be used by parents, caregivers and professionals as they use stories therapeutically to support children's mental and emotional health.

Other books in the series include:

- *The Waves: For Children Living With OCD*
- *The Sky Fox: For Children With Feelings Of Loneliness*
- *The Night Crossing: A Lullaby For Children On Life's Last Journey*
- *The Storm: For Children Growing Through Parents' Separation*
- *The Island: For Children With A Parent Living With Depression*
- *Storybook Manual: An Introduction To Working With Storybooks Therapeutically And Creatively*

Into The Forest – part of the *Therapeutic Fairy Tales* series – is born out of a creative collaboration between Pia Jones and Sarah Pimenta.

Pia Jones is an author, workshop facilitator and UKCP integrative arts psychotherapist, who trained at The Institute for Arts in Therapy & Education. Pia has worked with children and adults in a variety of school, health and community settings. Core to her practice is using arts and story as support during times of loss, transition and change, giving a TEDx talk on the subject. She was Story Director on artgym's award-winning film documentary, 'The Moving Theatre,' where puppetry brought to life real stories of people's migrations. Pia also designed the 'Sometimes I Feel' story cards, a Speechmark therapeutic resource to support children with their feelings. www.silverowlartstherapy.com.

Sarah Pimenta is an experienced artist, workshop facilitator and lecturer in creativity. Her specialist art form is print-making, and her creative practice has brought texture, colour and emotion into a variety of environments, both in the UK and abroad. Sarah has over 20 years' experience of designing and delivering creative, high-quality art workshops in over 250 schools, diverse communities and public venues, including the British Library, V&A, NESTA, Oval House and many charities. Her work is often described as art with therapeutic intent, and she is skilled in working with adults and children who have access issues and complex needs. Sarah is known as Social Fabric: www.social-fabric.co.uk.

Both Pia and Sarah hope these *Therapeutic Fairy Tales* open up conversations that enable children and families' own stories and feelings to be seen and heard.

Therapeutic Fairy Tales

Pia Jones and Sarah Pimenta

This unique therapeutic book series includes a range of beautifully illustrated and sensitively written fairy tales to support children experiencing challenging feelings and life situations, as well as a manual designed to support the therapeutic use of story.

Titles in the series include:
Storybook Manual: Working With Storybooks Therapeutically And Creatively
pb: 978-0-367-49117-8 / 2021

The Night Crossing: A Lullaby For Children On Life's Last Journey
pb: 978-0-367-49120-8 / 2021

The Island: For Children With A Parent Living With Depression
pb: 978-0-367-49198-7/ 2021

The Storm: For Children Growing Through Parents' Separation
pb: 978-0-367-49196-3 / 2021

Into The Forest: For Children With Feelings Of Anxiety
pb: 978-1-032-44927-2 / 2023

The Waves: For Children Living With OCD
pb: 978-1-032-44925-8 / 2023

The Sky Fox: For Children With Feelings Of Loneliness
pb: 978-1-032-44922-7 / 2023

These books are also available to purchase in sets:
Therapeutic Fairy Tales
pb: 978-0-367-25108-6 / 2021

Therapeutic Fairy Tales, Volume 2
pb: 978-1-032-11955-7 / 2023

Into The Forest

For Children With Feelings Of Anxiety

Pia Jones and Sarah Pimenta

Designed cover image: Sarah Pimenta

First published 2023
by Routledge
4 Park Square, Milton Park, Abingdon, Oxon OX14 4RN

and by Routledge
605 Third Avenue, New York, NY 10158

Routledge is an imprint of the Taylor & Francis Group, an informa business

© 2023 Pia Jones and Sarah Pimenta

The right of the authors to be identified as authors of this work has been asserted in accordance with sections 77 and 78 of the Copyright, Designs and Patents Act 1988.

All rights reserved. No part of this book may be reprinted or reproduced or utilised in any form or by any electronic, mechanical, or other means, now known or hereafter invented, including photocopying and recording, or in any information storage or retrieval system, without permission in writing from the publishers.

Trademark notice: Product or corporate names may be trademarks or registered trademarks, and are used only for identification and explanation without intent to infringe.

British Library Cataloguing-in-Publication Data
A catalogue record for this book is available from the British Library

Library of Congress Cataloging-in-Publication Data
Names: Jones, Pia, author. | Pimenta, Sarah, illustrator.
Title: Into the forest : for children with feelings of anxiety / Pia Jones
  and Sarah Pimenta.
Description: New York : Routeldge, 2023. | Series: Therapeutic fairy tales
  ; 7 | Audience: Ages 3-8. | Audience: Grades 2-3. | Summary: A wise owl
  teaches an anxious boy how to live in the present rather than fear the
  future.
Identifiers: LCCN 2022053159 (print) | LCCN 2022053160 (ebook) | ISBN
  9781032449272 (paperback) | ISBN 9781003374558 (ebook)
Subjects: CYAC: Anxiety--Fiction. | Owls--Fiction. | LCGFT: Picture books.
Classification: LCC PZ7.1.J726 In 2023 (print) | LCC PZ7.1.J726 (ebook) |
  DDC [E]--dc23
LC record available at https://lccn.loc.gov/2022053159
LC ebook record available at https://lccn.loc.gov/2022053160

ISBN: 978-1-032-44927-2 (pbk)
ISBN: 978-1-003-37455-8 (ebk)

DOI: 10.4324/9781003374558

Typeset in Calibri
by Deanta Global Publishing Services, Chennai, India

Printed in the UK by Severn, Gloucester on responsibly sourced paper

Acknowledgements

A special thank you to Stuart Lynch for all the time and creative support he generously gave to *Into The Forest*. A huge thanks also to Tamsin Cooke, Caroline Bailey, Katrina Hillkirk, Antonella Mancini, Molly Wolfe, Louise Higgs and Jo Parker for their insights on first readings. Thanks also to our families and friends for putting up with our absences so patiently while we worked on this series of books.

Thanks also to all the children and adults we have worked with across the years who have helped inspire us.

Thanks to the Speechmark team for all their support of our stories and turning them into such beautiful books. A special mention must go to Clare Ashworth for her enthusiasm and creative guidance. Her eagle eye came in handy too! And to Molly Kavanagh, Cathy Henderson and Alison Jones for taking our books into production with such care and attention. Our stories always felt in very safe hands.

Hello there,

Thank you for choosing to read our therapeutic fairy tale, *Into The Forest*. We hope that our story is useful in helping explore feelings of anxiety as well as giving ideas for support.

Sometimes it can seem like the more attention we give to our fears, the worse we feel. We can also worry that if we share our real feelings, other people can become worried too. We hope that *Into The Forest* opens up opportunities to have conversations about the anxiety we can all feel.

Learning to sit with our feelings, without judging or trying to fix them, can be a challenge for everyone, both children and adults. A trusted person, able to hear us fully, whatever we are feeling, can be a real help. There's an increasing understanding that nature can also play a role in calming and supporting us in times of stress, an idea now proven by studies in science.

We hope that you enjoy meeting our characters in nature and the forest.

Warmest wishes,

Pia & Sarah

Once upon a time, there was a Boy who lived at the edge of a town before the forest began. After school, the Boy loved to show off football moves to friends and teach his brother tricks on his bike.

If the Boy ever fell, he simply bit his lip and picked himself up. All the townsfolk admired him and said so:

"What a hardy child. What a 'strong fella' he will turn out to be."

Despite what everyone said, inside the Boy an uncomfortable feeling was growing. At times, it crept into his stomach, fizzy and tense. At other times, it gripped his chest, making his heart skip a beat. A force of its own, this feeling travelled around his body and made his mind race.

What if I can't do my wheelie at school today? Is my friend being off with me? Did I say something wrong? What if I don't get on the football team? What if I'm not strong after all?
What if people find out? What if? What if!

The Boy tried hard to pretend he was fine. Besides, he already knew what grown-ups would say:

Don't worry. Just stay positive. Show us how resilient you are!

Sometimes their advice worked, and sometimes it did not. It was in the quiet times that his feelings grew worse.

Before bedtime, the Boy's head became so noisy, his thoughts ran away with him and stopped him sleeping.

What if there is something wrong with me? What if? What if!

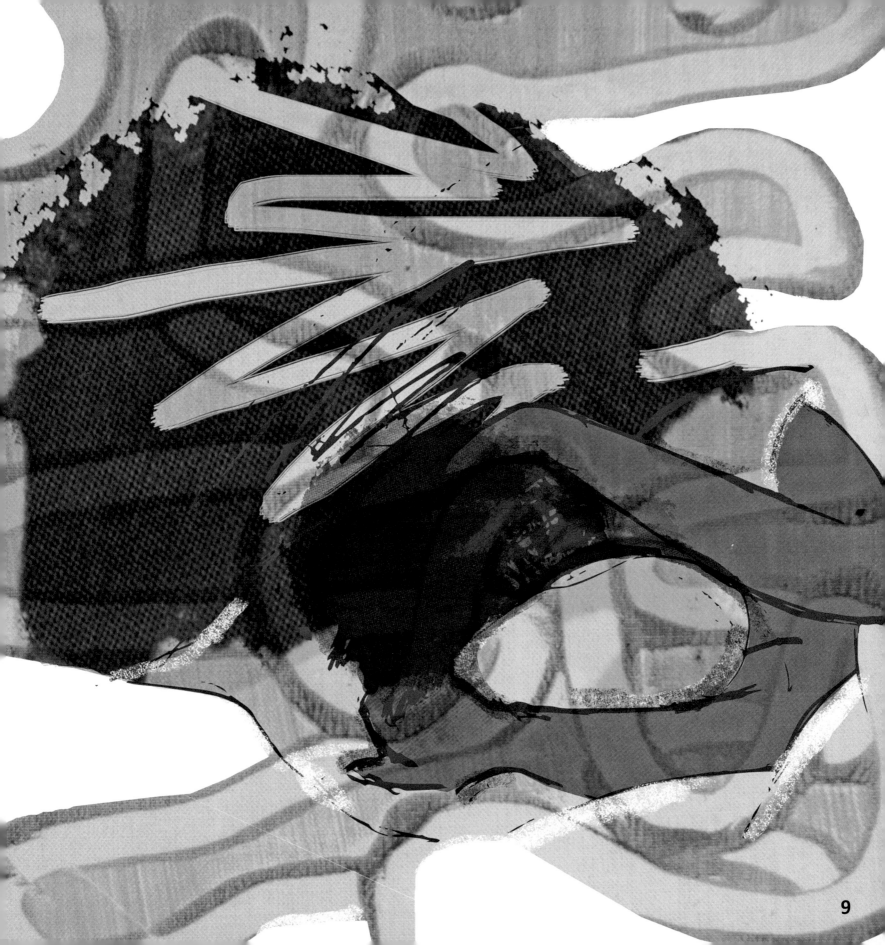

One day after school, the Boy took his bike out for a ride. Longing to clear his mind, he rode towards the forest.

Beyond a tall gateway of trees lay a lone path, one that he'd not seen before.

Lost in thought, the Boy cycled down the path, giant pine-trees passing in a blur. The speed of his spinning wheels matched the whir in his head.

What if... what if... what if!

As the Boy sped ever faster, he had the strangest sensation. The wheels on his bike were no longer spinning but rocking. Looking down, he stifled a cry. Was he *leaping*?

The Boy came crashing to a halt. Gone were his hands, feet and bicycle wheels. In their place stood four long furry legs and hooves. In his shock, the Boy could barely breathe.

"Oh my," said a slow, calm voice. "That is a change."

Spinning around, the Boy saw a grey Owl with gentle, golden eyes, perched on a nearby branch.

"Are you hurt?" it asked kindly, fluttering closer.

The Boy stumbled and cried out, "You can talk!"

"And hoot," added the Owl helpfully.

"What's going on? Who are you?" asked the Boy. "What's happening to me?"

"Ah," said the Owl. "You've wandered into the Forest of *What If*, where anything can happen. You've turned into a Deer; a Stag, if I'm not mistaken."

"I can't stay like this," cried the Boy. "How do I change back? I must get home to my family!"

"There is a way." The Owl shuffled along the branch nearer to the Boy. "I can help."

"What way?" demanded the Boy. "Please tell me!"

"There are three tasks. Complete them all to set yourself free. I'll be right here by your side."

"How do I begin?" said the Boy urgently, ears twitching.

"Your first task," explained the Owl, "is to take your time, and whisper *all* your worries to the wind ... old and new ... let the forest carry them for a while."

The Boy stared at the Owl. It wasn't easy to voice such things when they had been stewing inside for so long.

Lifting his head, the Boy began to whisper.

"What if I am no good? "What if nobody likes me?" "What if?"

Words tumbled out, one after the other. From a whisper, his voice gathered strength. As the Boy let go of his worries, his body gave a giant shudder.

"How hard for you," sighed the Owl when the Boy had finished. "What a lot of troubles to carry all on your own. How brave of you to share them."

The Boy felt a flicker of surprise. He'd never thought of bravery being anything like this.

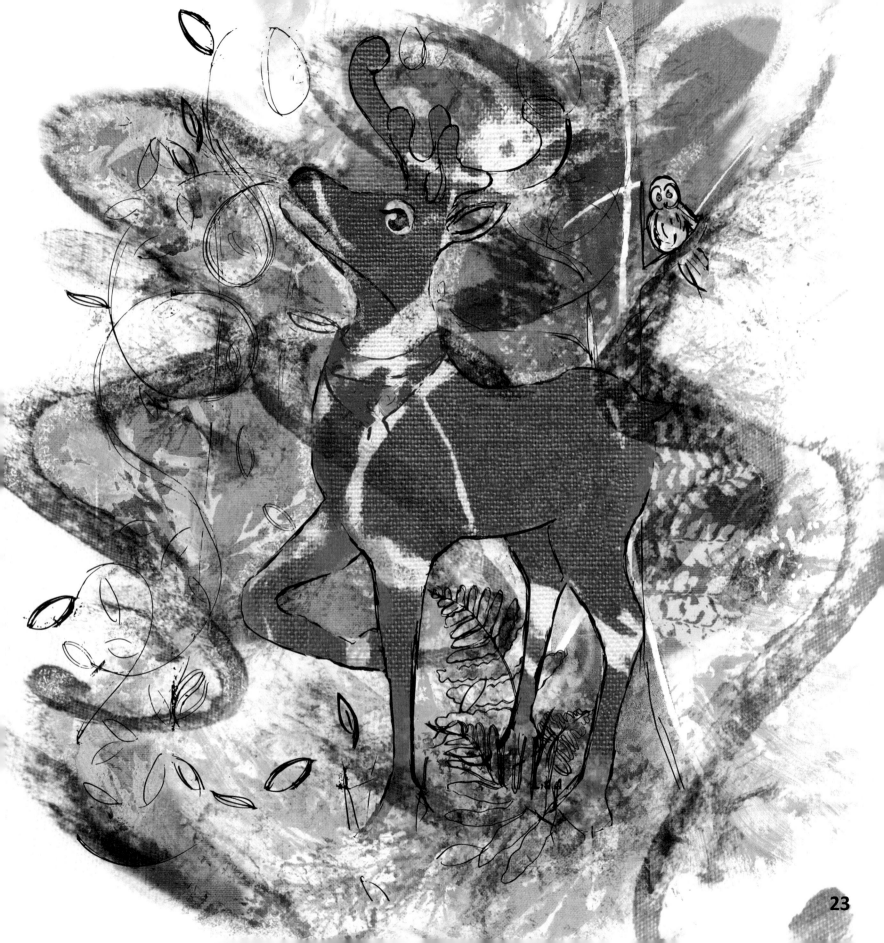

23

"Now that you've cleared your head," said the Owl gently, "your second task is to notice where you are standing and give the Forest *all* your attention. What do you see, smell, hear?"

The Boy followed the Owl's gaze and was struck by how light shone through the forest, turning the air gold. Trees towered majestically above him, roots draped in moss. As he sniffed at leaves, the Boy felt his senses wake up. The smell of pines tickled his nose. Birds chattered and swooped.

As he breathed it all in, the colours, sounds, smells filled him with a strange sense of awe. Feeling his own life force flow back into him, the Boy stamped the ground. His hooves struck the earth; wet, dark and solid.

"There you go," said the Owl, eyes twinkling. "Now that you are fully present in body and mind, are you ready for your third and final task?"

The Boy listened carefully as the Owl spoke; "Walk through the forest, as slowly as you can, and find a safe and special place to rest."

Taking his time, the Boy stepped through the forest, feeling the sun and shade take turns on his back. Leaves rustled and ferns swayed. The Boy's breath turned slow and steady. Finally, he reached an ancient, beautiful tree.

"This space feels safe and special," said the Boy to the Owl.

Taking shelter under its branches, the Boy rested against the tree. Somehow, it felt like his worries were held here too. He let out the deepest of sighs.

"It feels good to slow down, to hold this stillness," said the Boy. "It helps me know that I am a part of nature too. Like feelings can pass through me."

"Yes, and look what you've done," said the Owl triumphantly, with a sweep of his wing. "You've turned the Forest of *What If* back into its rightful state – the present – the *Forest of Here-and-Now*."

"What's that?" asked the Boy, blinking.

"You've tuned into the Forest and given it all your attention. *Here-and-Now* is the place for thoughts and feelings to come alive; that way we can listen and learn to be with them."

"Here-and-now," said the Boy, and grinned as he stretched open his hands. "So, I'm a boy again."

"Yes." The Owl's eyes shone. "Now you can take these ways back home to support yourself."

"It's true," agreed the Boy. "Today, I've learnt how to cope with my feelings a little bit more."

The Boy took a few deep breaths, enjoying the fresh air fill his chest. The earth felt solid beneath his feet.

"It's been a pleasure to meet you." The Owl started to flap his wings. "Now it's time for us both to go home. Goodbye."

"Thank you," said the Boy, waving. "Goodbye."

As the Owl flew away, the Boy noticed his bike by a tree. Smiling, he jumped on and pulled a long wheelie. As he rode along the path, the Boy took in the life around him. He knew now that, wherever he might be, he could use this way of being and breathing to help bring him back to the *Here-and-Now*.

A final word

Did you know that connecting with nature has been proven to help us feel calmer, more grounded and safer inside ourselves? Have you ever had a moment where you've found a special, safe place? Like the Boy in our story, sometimes it can help to stay still and allow ourselves to sense the natural world around us.

The ancient Japanese tradition, *Shinrin-yoku*, Forest Bathing, of being mindful and present amongst trees (with mobile devices or phones switched off, on silent or put away) has now travelled to many countries. Scientists have proven that trees release invisible chemicals called phytoncides (wood essential oils) that boost our health and immune system, relaxation and well-being. That wonderful smell of pine trees is actually doing wonders for our body! Equally, evidence shows that chemicals in the earth and soil are also having a calming effect on our body. Some people find the sound of water, rivers or seas calming too.

As many of us live in towns and cities, finding a safe corner in nature can work well. Please make sure that if you do explore any woods, gardens, parks, streams, rivers and seas, you stay safe, that there are trusted people nearby, and/or people know where you have gone. And if you don't have access to nature, looking at pictures can also help too!

Your teachers and parents/caregivers can find out more about the idea of nature as a support for well-being in our book *Rewilding Children's Imaginations*, which is packed full of creative ideas of how to connect with nature in fun, safe ways, through art making, storytelling and folktales.

We hope that you can find nature a support, be it a small corner or large spaces.

Pia & Sarah

Therapeutic Fairy Tales Volume 2:

Therapeutic Fairy Tales Volume 1:

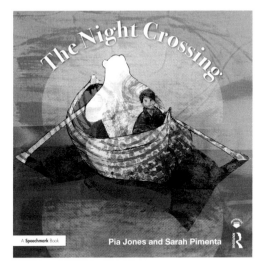

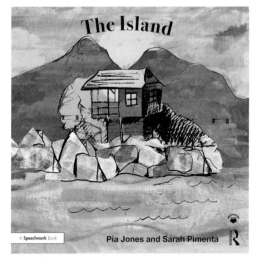